YOU SOLD YOUR COMPANY

Envisioning The Changes

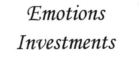

Emotions

Investments

Future Expectations

YOU SOLD YOUR COMPANY

Envisioning The Changes

Emotions

Investments

Future Expectations

J. TED OAKLEY

KEYSAR PUBLISHING COMPANY

KP

Library of Congress Catalog Card Number: 97-72363

ISBN: 0-9656287-4-4

Direct all inquiries to
Keysar Publishing Company
J.T.O.
2930 Denver Avenue
Corpus Christi, TX 78404

To Alice, Keys, Sarah,
Frank, and Phoebe

All good friends.

Contents

Introduction

Twenty years ago I met my first business owner who sold a company. I was intrigued with that person and enjoyed the exact and defined business style of this former owner. I knew immediately that the business owner type was the perfect match for my investing criteria. I was extensively trained in the investment planning business, but my business owner customers taught me more than I taught them. At the outset, little did I know that this entire group of people would become a study for me over the next twenty years. I learned more and more from these successful entrepreneurs with each passing month. I never realized the amount of respect I would eventually have for them. They would become great teachers for me over time.

When listening to the general public speak of "business owners" or "bosses," I am always surprised at how little they really know about the business owner. This entrepreneurial group of people is very misunderstood. Owners and former owners of businesses are the lifeblood of this country. They take the most risk, pay the most tax, and help the most people. Yet they often receive very negative media coverage and are the least appreciated in most cases among all types of business employees, professionals, executives, and others. As a group, they are very benevolent and philanthropic. Who funds most of the charities and endorsements in this country? They are former business owners who

sold their companies. The need to give back something to their country and community was paramount
in their minds. Obviously, in the long run, it wasn't
strictly the money.

As you read this book, I hope to take you through
a time-line beginning with the day you sold your company. The different types of people who sold their businesses and the variety of emotions they experienced are
incorporated herein. Whether you sold for $1 million
or $100 million, I think the information will benefit the
thought process. The path after selling is going to have
some unexpected curves and potholes. Unexpected
emotions will arise. The business owner who sells the
company will also be able to bridge the gap between
thinking of helping others and really doing it. Watch-
ing this wonderful world unfold for someone you have
helped is a powerful feeling.

The changes that take place after selling a business can only be experienced. I have counseled with
thousands of business owners who knew little of what

emotions to anticipate. They had to experience this firsthand. Maybe this book will shorten the time span between selling the business and experiencing the changes.

The examples given here are real people with only the names changed. I have chosen to use the third-person singular "he" (where applicable), rather than "he or she", in order to avoid repetition. This decision in no way reflects any gender preference among readers. These examples range from 30 states to almost 100 different kinds of businesses. They include people who lost their fortunes to those who went on to become incredibly wealthy. If you have sold a business, many of the thoughts will probably make an impression.

As you go forward, remember to be thankful that you are in one of the most unique groups of people. The thrill of being able to build and sell a business, is not experienced by many people. As you cross the threshold from owning a business to selling a business, many changes will occur. We hope these next chapters will help you see them for what they are: Success!

I

Closing Day

You have just signed the papers for selling your company. By tomorrow morning the cash will be in your bank or the stock certificates in your hands. You pause to reflect on how it began and how it ended.

You could be the person in California who borrowed $25,000 on credit cards to start a business which is now worth $15,000,000. You could be the person who bought the small company from his dad and built it into $100,000,000. You could be the hourly worker who decided to do it on his own and ended up with $2,000,000.

Basically, all the stories are the same. The players change and the size of the company varies. However, one thing remains constant: Great feelings of accomplishment are soon interrupted. The tribe from the acquiring company arrive to take over: the lawyers, the CPAs, the bean counters — all of them. Now they are telling you what will be happening. "This is your new regional manager." "We've decided to move your office down the hall." Your reactions range from "Was this the right thing to do?" to "I feel like an orphan."

How did you end up here? Why did you sell the company? You probably were motivated by one of three elements: succession, expansion, profit. The lack of a clear successor is one of the primary reasons. A father realizes his children are not interested in running the business. Or the owner has no children or people in the company who are capable of running it. This business must be sold while the owner is still in full command in order to gain the most.

A second reason is the inability to gain capital for expansion. Almost every business reaches this point along the way. The owner can overcome the capital problem at certain points, but then the risk becomes too great of losing it all just to expand. He decides to sell. If he sees consolidation in the industry and waits too long, the price goes down. If he sees consolidation coming and sells too soon, money is left on the table.

The third reason for selling is simply because the offering price was too high to resist. As a business owner, he knew what the business was worth. He may even have known within a time frame that the business would start to decline. If someone offers more than the business is worth under any circumstances, the owner has to sell. This is especially true when public stock companies come calling. If two or three are bidding against each other, the price can become ridiculous.

For the business owner who has sold the company, many changes will take place during the next five years — more than he cares to admit or can even envision. Every company is created to sell at some point, either to a buyer or to the public market. Like acorns into trees and back to earth, everything has a cycle.

Most business owners are blind to the future after selling. They have spent the last five to fifteen years of their life focused on running their company. It's not over; actually, things are just starting. However, this is the watershed event, a turning point, and life after the sale is new territory to be explored. This book gives insight into what some of this territory will be.

Business owners are a totally different breed from employees. They have more guts, less fear, more definition, determination, and self confidence than persons lacking the entrepreneurial spirit and drive. Their world changes after the sale, since most believe the replacement executives cannot manage the businesses nearly as efficiently as the founders. But that's life. When they sell their companies, they also sell the power. Can they live with that? In the following pages we will discover varied individual reactions.

II

The New Routine

The new routine is a very interesting time for the former business owner. Usually this period is like a honeymoon. Much time is spent getting to know all the players from the acquiring company in lunches, sessions, and meetings, with nothing particularly notable to determine. Everyone's best foot is being put forward and potential conflicts are being minimized. The new company may be introducing its acquisition as the new great addition. The former owner probably senses, even this early, that problems could arise, but the honeymoon feeling makes him say — "We'll work it out."

Business owners are by nature optimistic. They have a tendency in early months to assume the kinks will go away. "We will discuss the problems and find solutions, with little compromises on my part." Sometimes this is the case, but more times than not — what the former owner confronts are subtle changes in management style and direction.

The new routine affects the spouse as well, especially if the spouse was used to having all the "small costs" and odd jobs absorbed by the company. All of the marginal benefits of owning a business suddenly vanish. Company-paid insurance, car washes and maintenance, errands, clean-ups, parties, trips, and car phones are but a few of the give-ups. I have visited many business owners' offices and realized the importance a spouse has when she walks in and everyone knows this is the owner's other half, also known as the "boss." The same is true for male spouses when the woman owns the business. Generally all fringe benefits are gone after the sale of the company.

At the beginning, everyone assumes that all will end well. Naturally everyone wants to believe this. I am constantly shown how many business owners do not understand what lies ahead. The standard comment is "we" are going to do this, and "we" are going to do that, denying that "we" no longer exists. They haven't yet truly realized that they are now working for someone else.

Morris K. was an interesting Midwest owner who sold his business in the early 1980's. I met with him soon after the sale, and he had a most upbeat attitude about how everything was going to be great. The acquiring company had promised him the option to expand the business and do well for himself also. However, each time I visited him, he had become less and less enthusiastic.

I have a standard warning to business owners: If you sell your company and agree to be employed by the acquiring company, don't be overly optimistic. Eight out of ten times it does not work. Morris K. was in this situation and failed to recognize it. After the initial phase wore off, he was shocked. Fifteen months later he was in Florida, with only vague memories of how it was supposed to be.

The new routine impacts your customers also. They see the announcement and notice the transfer to different bank accounts. They are shaken, and you assure them that nothing will change. You are trying to convince yourself and them that this is true — but instinctively you know it is not. After all, no one can take care of your customers the way you do. This is precisely why you have done so well.

All of the new routine is taking place while your primary asset (cash or stock) is sitting there doing nothing. You realize that this major reinvestment problem can be taken care of later. Maybe.

III

Life After Selling

Every business owner feels partially lost after selling their company, a very normal reaction. When he assumes the "ex" or "former" status and starts groping around, trying to find out what to do with himself the morning after selling, he's not alone. Every former owner is in some way doing the same thing. From my years of experience, I can offer many observations that could help these retired owners in making the difficult adjustments.

First and most important, they must adopt a realistic and pragmatic attitude. Yes, they *have* been successful — perhaps very successful — in founding and managing one or more business enterprises and coping with a variety of financial, marketing, and other challenges. The emphasis here is on the past tense. There is no guarantee that they will succeed in other entrepreneurial-investment undertakings in the future. Business owners as a group, with naturally large egos, never consider failure as an option. Some have a tendency to act hastily and compulsively to organize or gain control of another company in services, marketing, or manufacturing without adequate financial backup or expertise to make it prosper. I can say, from my observations and knowledge, that such impulsive financial decisions have a major potential for disaster.

This does not mean that former owners should not look for other businesses. But they must also be patient, patient, patient! Their friends and family are constantly saying "What are you going to do with your life?" The answer is simply "I have not decided on anything." The best choice with the best reward-to-risk ratio will appear in time. The former owner will have the gut feeling that the price and the operations available for him constitute an opportunity he cannot turn down.

Examples of two individuals who sold and then reacted in different ways come to mind. Tom W. was a business owner who sold a company in the Southeast and immediately decided to go out and buy a NASCAR racing company. He had never been in the racing business and merely enjoyed the sport. Over the next three years he lost his entire nest egg and never made his racing business successful. He had been set for life and is now back working to make it again.

Tim P., on the other hand, sold his company to a public corporation and waited until the right situation presented itself. He moved slowly and within two years started another company somewhat related to his old. Two years later, he has an organization that is larger than the original. He is still expanding and very happy. The key was waiting for the right time.

Second, I strongly recommend that a business owner who liquidates set up an office away from his residence. Get a real office! Now after ten, twenty, or more years with his company, he is without management responsibility and he brings all of his office paraphernalia home with him. Does he really think his spouse wants him home twenty-four hours a day? Maybe at age 65, but not now. He has all of his phones, computers, faxes, and nowhere to go. He has business meetings in the living area. The family answering machine is filled with messages. The spouse will usually be very frustrated but will live with it.

The greatest benefit of an office for the former owner is quiet time. He is at a point where reflection on his life and his situation is very important. Having a place to go and a routine are both very healthy after selling.

Moreover, the former owner should avoid self-conversion into a professional investor. Just because a newly acquired fortune provides easy access to stock, bond, real estate, and option and derivative markets, it does not rank the inexperienced as a great investor. Jim T. was a good friend and client who obtained a stock quote machine and all the programs to run his *new* investment business. Actually, he knew very little about investing. He forgot that investing is a unique sphere with many risks along with the rewards.

In the beginning, he traded, bought, sold, and tried his hand. When visiting him the next year, I asked in general about his investments. His reply was that he never turned the equipment on anymore. He realized his job was to determine how much of his money to allocate to various types of investment vehicles, making sure he understood the risks. Having done that, he then knew that his area of expertise lay not in making money by investing, but in finding capable money managers whom he could be confident would do the job for him (i.e., reach his investment goals).

Passive investing through professional managers can look easy. In reality there are very few people like Warren Buffett or George Soros in the investment business. Investing assets is a much slower process than most people think. Of course patience is very important, but it is only one of many requisites in this increasingly complex and constantly changing field. Former owners interested in active investments must wait for the right business to come along. Their prior experience should prove valuable in making this selection.

Last but not least, the active or direct investor, in founding a new enterprise or investing funds in one which is on-going, must be a shrewd investigator of, and a careful listener to knowledgeable sources. He must realize that investing in another business first requires tedious and detailed scrutiny of the target. If he starts calling all his business friends and deal-makers, they may conclude that he is pressing to own another company quickly. Corporate finance and deal people will show up all over the place.

Now is the time for ex-owners to start listening carefully. Their best opportunity can come from being around business. They should stay close to active business owners in as many areas of operations as possible. These corporate officers are often the first to learn when a business is going to be on the block. Potential buyers who were former owners should not overlook any enterprise available for purchase which has potential. They should indeed look at everything, but take the time to watch very carefully and to stay in tune with related, critical economic and financial developments. In time, a situation will present itself and they will recognize it.

The best business buyers and starters I have observed are very slow to commit capital. But when the right deal appears, they move quickly. This may take a number of years. The active ingredient they all possess

is the ability to listen well. They remember that they
have plenty of time.

IV

Reality Check

Reality after the sale of a business comes in different packages. The business owner who stays with the new company has one type of new reality, the business owner who retires, or thinks he can, has another; whereas the business owner who has multiple companies experiences very little change after selling only one of them.

The business owner who stays with the company usually takes a needed vacation, pays off debt, or contemplates the next step. I'm amazed at how many business owners are surprised that the marriage of the two companies is not going as they had planned. Big corporations buy smaller companies in order to control, grow, and run the new entity. They bought — you sold! Very few corporations are run well enough to allow the prior owner to join in the decision (growth) phase. Too many egos, too much power, too many bean counters to do that.

Most entrepreneurial companies are more efficiently run than large or medium-sized corporations. Generally speaking, among the top five executives of these corporations, few, if any, have ever been threatened seriously by insecurity, had to meet payroll, or mortgaged their souls to make something happen. Hardly any executives have faced day-to-day fear of losing it all.

Lloyd T. was a client and former owner who sold to a public company. When we first started working together he was jubilant about the prospects of the new combination. I told him to be very circumspect because his company might have been managed more efficiently and cost effectively than the larger acquiring company. He was a great operator and, sure enough, the executive controllers of the mother company were afraid of him. He was a potential problem, from the standpoint of corporate political powers at the new headquarters he was serving, if in fact he was more skilled at managing the company he had founded than they were. As it happened, the company developed severe financial problems and he left. The reality of the situation took some time to set in place. This is a very normal occurrence.

The first sign of stress comes with accounting changes. One of the loyal employees of the former owner is going berserk over all the new accounting procedures enforced by the new home office.

The second sign of stress comes when a capital item needs to be purchased for a reasonably small sum. The former owner discovers that a thirty-year-old MBA insists that a request form has to be approved at regional headquarters. Meanwhile, he is confronted by a customer who is livid and probably on the verge of changing company suppliers.

The third sign of stress comes when the former owner realizes that the input of his ideas will mean little or nothing to the big corporation minds and "mind-set" which do not adjust easily to directing business on other than a grand scale. For most of them, it's politics as usual.

V

"I'm a Consultant to the New Company..."

How many times have I heard the above statement, only to realize the former business owner does not understand "consulting." When a corporation buys a company it has an agenda in mind. The former owner is put into a consulting role for one of three reasons:

First, the buy-out is structured so that part of the price is a consulting arrangement for compensation. This usually takes place because more money is needed to close the transaction. The former owner in reality does little or no consulting. As a matter of fact, the acquiring company does not even bother to call. People ask what the person is doing and the euphemism "consulting" pops up.

Second, the acquiring company does not have the ability to admit they cannot release the owner. They really do not want him and do not plan on keeping him, but just cannot tell him. The acquiring company usually wants to get the deal underway and make a smooth transition.

An example of this from 1987 comes to mind: Robert D. was a business owner who lived in the Midwest but sold his company to a publicly owned concern in Texas. He was classified as a consultant as well as a director. In many public companies, power and politics are more important than making money. This was the case with Robert D. and the acquiring company. After four or five board meetings he realized that "consulting" meant nothing. They were never going to listen to him or change their ideas on any subject. At the beginning of his second year the company bought out his contract and he left.

I am also reminded of Scotty G. in Memphis whose business was acquired by a public company which put him on consultant status. The company wanted him to consult with their merger/acquisition manager when potential new companies were being acquired. After Scotty visited two of the potential acquisition candidates, he concluded that they should not be bought due to lack of quality in many areas. Obviously this put the merger/acquisition manager in an unusual position. Three months later Scotty's contract was purchased and he was a consultant no more.

Third, when a company has been acquired, the former owner will consult in order to retain the top customers. For example, Wallace B. owned a company in Denver that was sold to a public company. He had three clients who represented a large portion of his service business. The acquiring company made him a consultant in order to keep these customers. The former owner had no office, only his home. When two of the three customers left, the acquiring company said goodbye to Wallace.

Consulting is very hard for the former business owner. He is neither in nor out but usually in a misleading and temporary limbo. If a business owner sells his company and works directly for the new company, the rules are clear. He must do what upper management tells him to do. This is usually a managerial assignment, not a consulting position. In some cases, the owner's status is actually much clearer by being an employee instead of a consultant. One thing is certain — the new company will run operations differently from the former owner.

The former owner should keep consulting in perspective and negotiate the most favorable financial terms for his contract. At best, it is a stop-gap measure before he does something else. The period spent at this position may be one to three years, but eventually the former owner moves on, either by his own choice or by the decision of the new management. Consulting to the new company always sounds better than it works in real life.

VI

Family Relationships After the Sale

After the business is sold, a myriad of changes affecting the family will take place. These changes will be confined to two major areas – work and home. Both will need to be reviewed for signs of stress.

In the workplace, the essential family adjustment will depend on which family members were involved in the business sold. In the event it was built and managed by a married team with the principal owner working full-time and the other spouse at a fifty percent part-time or higher level, a serious family problem may arise. If the purchaser retains the former owner in some capacity, this is usually the only contract he signs with the top management of the acquisition. The spouse who is turned away generally receives no monetary compensation or other recognition of his (her) contributions over an extended span of time. A radically altered life-style inevitably unfolds for this couple. Whether they enjoy this change depends on each specific situation and of course the personalities.

John and Bonnie were a couple in the west that had a thriving and very special niche business. When their company was purchased, the acquiring corporation kept John but not Bonnie. Bonnie was the guiding force in this company, the person to whom most of the employees turned for guidance. She was more or less the glue that bonded the acquisition.

The offering price was so generous that neither Bonnie nor John could turn it down. Unfortunately, the business suffered greatly due to the change, but the new owners, who employed John, never identified the reason. Had they retained her services as well as John's, the business would probably have continued its established pattern of earnings growth.

Many issues will face the business owner and spouse after the sale and most of the problems will be emotional in nature. If children were involved in the business sold, another complete set of issues is encountered. The more children that were employed, the greater the problems. If the acquiring company elects not to keep any or all children as employees, new careers must be generated. If the acquiring company chooses to employ only one of the children, this can cause family tensions and discord. Needless to say, a host of disruptive forces can be unleashed in the family circle.

Ben C. owned a southeast business that employed three of his children. All were granted positions with the new company after the sale. Three years later, two of the children had been terminated and the third was moved to a different site. Ben was disgruntled with the company for breaking up his family work unit. If the truth were known, he did not have the capability to do what should have been done in the beginning — not to have hired them when he organized his company or encouraged them to seek alternative employment at the time of the sale.

Within the home, family members experience an entirely different set of issues. What used to be the routine for a family that owned the business is funda-mentally changed. The family members do not go to work at exactly the same time, come home at the same time, or even meet as a family at the same time. When a business owner employs family members, a different mindset is in place. Salaries and draws are different from the practices of publicly traded corporations and a closely built family hierarchy is usually developed. Having observed the sale of numerous family businesses, I have also noted that many of these families will separate afterwards. Each member has his own measure of financial independence and wants something different in life. This is not necessarily bad, but it can lead to radical changes in family relations over a period of time.

The major family problems arise when the owner of the business tries to help support other family members – usually children – after the sale. In my opinion, this is an absolute recipe for disaster. If a business owner is trying to support two or three families in addition to his own, the assets will need to be very large. I have witnessed five to fifteen million dollars shrink very rapidly when three or four families were depending totally or largely on such amounts for support. And of course as the principal shrinks so does the ordinary income generated by that principal.

Cecil Y. and his wife sold a great business in California and had enough money to last their entire lifetime and more. The cash flow that they were generating from investments was very large. As they moved along in time, each child started using Mom and Dad to maintain his or her life-style. Over time, I met on several occasions with the parents in an effort to make them understand that their own life-style could be in jeopardy and might inevitably require a radical reduction of periodic family subsidies. My counsel was ignored and, over the long run, the children squandered most of the balance of the fortune.

This unfortunate result happened because the parents were not able to tell their children, "You need to make your own money and provide for your own financial security and independence." Actually, the children were robbed of the chance to make it on their own merits and win self-confidence and respect. In the end, everyone was damaged. This family financial tragedy occurs and recurs repeatedly. So what does the owner do?

If the business owner has children or a spouse in the business, think about the consequences of selling. As much as possible, let everyone in the family know how his or her life will or will not change after the sale, especially in a financial way. They may or may not have jobs. Their salaries may or may not be the same. If possible, make sure that the mature children know in advance that they are on their own. If this is difficult to do, the former owner must tally the benefits. One may be saving his own new life-style. One benefit for sure will be his own mental health. The owner should make detailed plans for the use of the increased wealth, with emphasis on children *before* selling his company.

VII

The Big Risk

After selling the company, the former owner is now entering the most risky phase of the journey. This risky period is broken down into two parts: First, the period when the individual has been paid for the sale, next, the period when the seller is considering other deals in which to invest. Both of these areas can be devastating to the new-found wealth of the former business owner.

When the company is sold, the former owner now has liquidity as never before, which may be in the form of cash or stock in a public company. Due to the great advance in stock prices in the last decade, many public corporations are using stock for acquisitions. The former owner in this new status often has made no plans for reinvestment, and this period can bring the biggest risk the owner has ever taken. Most owners believe liquidity makes the situation conservative. What happens now is the need to keep pace with inflation, conserve assets, and be very defined. Bigger risk is involved now than when the person owned the business. A business owner is in control of the business and it is most likely that the business is growing.

Keeping pace with inflation is automatic. Whatever liquidity the business owner has is well cared for and defined. Business owners are in control of their business whether good or bad. This situation is in total contrast to having liquidity and *no control* over any selected investments. Explosions of investments happen at this stage. Bad timing, bad investments, and poorly thought-out ideas. Remember this — you are not in control. Everything you do must be thoroughly examined. If you make a mistake, there will be no turning back. When the company was yours, you could bounce back after hard times. Bouncing back is no longer an alternative when losses come after selling the business. You are now in the big risk arena. This is one situation not to take lightly.

The other part of the big risk time frame is investing in the next business or deal. Every former owner wants to invest in an idea that will make money. They thrive on doing the best deal. Most former owners did it very well in their own "deal." This is precisely why they are now wealthy. Only a fool will jump quickly to the next business without taking the time to examine it in detail. The single most common mistake by former business owners is to move too quickly. Why the rush? Does this person really need more money right now? I doubt it. They must analyze carefully all attractive options available.

There are thousands of deals out there that can make or break a person. Someone is always there to separate you from your money. People will be selling to you daily. Take time to decide how you feel about certain kinds of investments. Move slowly and get to know yourself again. You do not have to be in business immediately. Every salesperson will try to make you think this deal is the last "good one." More and more deals will come your way. Be patient and delight in looking at all of these. You are now in the big risk arena and not in control after the investment is made. Watch closely and do not jump quickly to the next deal.

VIII

Emptiness

Business owners get so caught up in the acquisition deal that everything else is forgotten. Somewhere in all the confusion is the heart of the seller. After all the hype and hoopla of the sale, the business owner walks away with millions of dollars in stock or cash. For the first time in his life, he is debt free, job free, and responsibility free.

From an outside point of view, the scenario would look like a complete no-lose situation. The company is sold. With adequate capital for a lifetime of total financial security and freedom, what more could any person ever want? This former successful entrepreneur is supposed to be on top of the world; but inside him there is often an emptiness, a lack of goals and purpose. The emptiness stems from once having all of everything to do and suddenly having all of nothing to do.

In many ways this stage of life is no different from graduating from high school. All your friends are going in different directions, attending different schools, and taking on different jobs. At first, you don't know exactly what you want to do. Somehow you decide, and off to some university or job you go. You're back on track. When you sell your company, all your friends are still running theirs, have jobs, etc. Somehow you will decide in this situation also.

Mike K. was an owner in the Northwest who sold his company and stayed on to run the business. His case is a great example of being heartbroken because the business was no longer his. He had only a high school education. This business had been his entire life! After selling, he was totally despondent and had tremendous seller's remorse. Running the business for someone else became so frustrating that he eventually quit and moved South. I don't think he was ever truly happy afterwards.

Getting out of college produces a similar feeling. You have reached a level that is now supposed to make you and everyone else very happy. But this concept is very hard to sell to a graduate who is twenty-three years old and jobless.

The business owner, after selling, often feels emotionally depressed. He expected this hour to be his happiest. However, a death of sorts has occurred, and he is in a period of mourning a profound loss — of purpose, focus, identity. A new part must be developed in order to regain these feelings. No spouse, second home, or extended travel will fulfill this loss. Why do they feel this way? This question is asked over and over again. They know that this hour should be their happiest.

In the mind of the business owner who sold the company, a lot of new thinking must and will take place. This will be a time to look at himself and truly take stock. What do I like most? What types of activities get me excited? Fishing, golfing, and tinkering only go so far. After some time, the person has to determine the importance of purpose and to analyze his personal concept of happiness.

IX

Staying, Leaving, or Starting Over

Staying with the company, leaving, or starting over is the next major decision. If the business owner is staying with the company the sequence goes like this:

No contract — only year-to-year agreement to stay on. This arrangement normally does not last.

Three-year contract — This gives both sides a chance to see each other in action. Some of these last and some do not.

Earn-out contract — This almost always works because the former owner and the company both have a vested interest towards increasing business.

If the decision to stay is taken, he must emotionally decide to settle in, relax and let someone else call the final shot. A number of business owners can do this, but overall it is a hard task for most. Business owners may stay due to net worth considerations, lack of energy to do it all over again, or just no attractive, alternative career opportunity.

Size of acquired assets — as well as personalities — are factors for most prior owners. The larger the deal, the less likely the person is to stay. It is difficult to imagine a prior owner worth $20 million taking orders from a regional manager earning $100,000 annually. Also, certain business owners cannot and will not work for someone again, no matter what the situation.

The business owner who considered staying but instead ended up leaving is in a very unusual position. Assets are in hand but there are no real plans. In my experience, this business owner is the one who must really spend some time getting in touch with himself. What do I want, what do I like, what makes me happy?

Business owners who know they are leaving must go through all the necessary steps to say good-bye. A day of reckoning finally arrives when they are in their new office with absolutely nothing to do but look at their investments. This is another person who must spend time "taking stock" of himself.

Business owners who sell their companies and plan to retire have a whole new set of problems. Only certain individuals can retire and be totally happy. Business owners got where they are by staying busy, building enterprises, and extracting deep satisfaction from the sense of accomplishment, and having fun.

Business owners who sell their company and plan on retiring are going through entrepreneurial "menopause." This retirement "thing" is nothing like they planned. All the hustle and bustle of management life vanishes in a few weeks. Their entire life changes dramatically. The spouse at home went through a big change when all the children left. He is going through his now.

Don B. was a business owner in the Midsouth who planned on retiring and living the "good life." He had bought a new home on the coast and decided to do more sailing, golfing, etc. He had not anticipated the magnitude of the change. Every time I spoke with him he was irate about something. His wife thought he was off balance, and he was making her miserable at home. Within the next two years he got involved in three other companies and all was well. Being ready to step away from the business world is a major decision. The mind has to be in perfect balance for this to happen.

Purpose in life is a much bigger item than most people realize. Adding input to a project, helping people, giving aid, assisting young workers — all give great feelings of purpose to a business owner. And beneath the surface, there is the ego which thrives on feeling indispensable.

The need to get an office, to move money around, to do something, to do anything is paramount. The retired owner's spouse is saying "Get an office." He shouldn't be at home all the time. He may be driving his spouse into spells of barely concealed exasperation as well. I can always tell when someone is retired when I'm managing assets for them. Phone calls concerning small subjects come in constantly. These people do not have enough to do. So they call the closest thing to business that they have, their money manager. On many occasions I have hoped they would find a job soon. It's almost as if everyone around the retired business owner knows it but himself. Wife, banker, children, CPA, investment advisor, broker, and attorney all realize the same thing. He needs a job!

The business owner who goes directly into another business is usually very happy. Little change takes place. There may be fewer employees and fewer problems, but a good focus on where they are going. Life for these people will probably get better with more simplification, while still realizing the fun of doing something worthwhile.

There was the case of Jon M. in Canada who sold his company to a U.S. corporation. He then immediately started another company and went full force into the business. Nothing changed. In fact, he was better at running the second company than the first. No remorse, no emotional changes, and no stress on the family due to having no purpose. Starting over in these situations is normally very healthy. As you can see, the decision to stay, leave, or start over can be a major hurdle.

X

100% or Nothing at All

Business owners will often sell one business and, after some time, reinvest in another one. One of the most nagging questions becomes – what level or percent of their time should they invest in the new business?

The most optimum scenario would be to own a company and spend 30% to 50% of their time with the new entity. This would allow the owners to enjoy the fruits from the sale of the first company, while having some goals to achieve and regular involvement in management decisions in the new venture. After toiling for many years to develop and sell the first business, the former owner usually does not want to become immediately locked into another. Obviously, he has the option to invest in a company, hire other officers to exercise daily oversight, but still retain chief executive control.

Unfortunately, in the real world, this does not usually happen. As a prior business owner, he knows that it rarely runs right — by his standards — without his being there. When their own money is not on the line, employees do not usually perform as an owner would. The owner is either the boss or not the boss. If his employees know he is not there most of the time, it has an impact. The organization that was sold had the former owner's style and flavor written all over it. If he is not there, no flavor exists.

Frank L. was a client in the northwest who sold an industrial company and shortly afterwards bought another company. He would fly into town and work at the company about 25% of the time. He became angry when employees either did not know that he was the owner or just did not treat him as such. All they knew was that his full-time manager signed their checks. In their eyes, the manager was the real boss. In theory, the part-time system sounds great but works very poorly in real life.

Jonathan D. was a great client who sold a company in the southwest and soon after bought another in California. His idea was to have a corporation providing reasonable income, to offset incidental expenses, and which would require a limited number of hours and no rigid schedule. When we reviewed his new management arrangement, he admitted the upsetting dilemma of entrapment in full-time employment. Within two years he had sold this company and was back to square one.

What does work? Two types of situations come to mind that I have observed to be satisfactory. If the former owner had a top-notch, long-time employee who knew the business very well, this could be a starting point. Two ingredients must be in place. The employee manager should be in the same type of business in the second venture as in the first. The employee should own at least a small percent of the new business. In this manner, the former owner can own controlling interest and not necessarily be there all the time. This is a great setup — if it works when implemented.

Allen B. was a client in the southeast who sold a company and retired, or so he thought. After searching four years for another business, he was unsuccessful in finding what he wanted. In the meantime, his former top manager and two supervisors contacted him to offer their services in a new business essentially the same as the old one. He accepted their proposal and the business worked like a dream. All of the key ingredients were there. Same business, same employees. The only difference being a very minor investment by the former owner. He did not bet the farm this second time around. He let the new management bear the strain of corporate expansion.

In a second type of situation that works, the former owner invests in two or three companies that he knows well and acts as a board member only. This has been a satisfactory arrangement for many investors. If they know the business and the people involved, then it has a chance of working. This allows former owners to invest, but still exercise potential influence on major corporate decisions. If the above conditions do not apply, great caution must be exercised.

Both of these scenarios are average at best. Not being 100% involved is a difficult role for a former business owner, even though the goal would be part-time management. More often than not, however, the investor/owner either has to become involved full-time, or not at all. You cannot just have your toe in the water. Typically, the former owner would like to run the business on 20-hour weeks. But he knows instinctively that the business world dictates more.

Actually most former owners are eventually happier if they return on a full-time basis. It is in their management blood stream, as they all know, and very hard to eliminate.

This is one more reason why a business owner should take time before going on to the next business. If the former owner is not prepared to put in the requisite time and other effort, then he should remain retired.

XI

What Have I Become?

After selling a company, most business owners select a direction or style of business activity based on personality. Over the last twenty years, I have noticed four different types of approach. In categorizing these sellers, I noticed they were like certain animals.

Business owners usually sell their company for cash, stock, notes, or a combination of all. The new-found wealth is either very liquid or semi-liquid. Post sellers all either invest conservatively or spend wildly, feeling their wealth unlimited.

The four categories of post sellers' personalities are: leap frog, butterfly, beaver, and lemming. The leap frog is the owner who sells the company but wants to go for more. He sells a company for five million but needs to have twenty-five million to feel he has "made it." This takes a big leap frog maneuver to do. Some entrepreneurs can do this but the risk is high. The person who made wealth in one business now has to try it in another. Many people have the mistaken idea that making the next leap will be easy.

Most leap frog types are very enthusiastic after selling a company. They see the huge windfall of making money with money, but in reality, most leap frogs will end up far less wealthy and dismayed over risky losses. For example, John J. was a former business owner who could have lived on the income from his investments. He personally signed notes for shopping centers, trying to increase his wealth. The notes were called, and he lost it all. He took a leap backward if anything. Mack S. was a fellow in the Midwest who sold a company and did turn two million dollars into fifteen million through buying and operating other companies. It can work both ways.

The butterfly is the owner who plowed all his assets back into the business. He wound the cocoon of assets over the years by keeping a very low profile economically. All of a sudden the business is sold and a spring-like atmosphere begins. The former owner and the spouse start to enjoy life a bit more, spend some money, and become a butterfly just released from the cocoon of ownership. I am always happy to see this type of owner really start to have some fun. He normally will invest in reasonably safe avenues and just enjoy the ride.

My favorite butterfly is Bill L. in the Midwest. He exchanged his company for stock in the acquiring firm, and, as luck would have it, the stock increased five hundred percent in price. Amazing! He then quit working and starting traveling. He gave money to his children, church and friends and made his life one big, enjoyable trip. He has continued to enjoy his money over all the years I have known him.

The beaver is the former owner who, after selling a company, stacks all of the proceeds of sale in the "money dam" and waits for winter to come. He tries to have everything in place for a potential catastrophe (all of the money hoarded for the rainy day). Most beavers forget that life is a journey — meant to be traveled, not placed on hold. Some beavers are happy, but others just feel safe and never really enjoy the fruits of many years of "sweat equity." Are they really happy? Many are not but continually look for the key to happiness in having "enough" assets.

Fred W. was my idea of the never-ending beaver saga. If you have ever watched beavers, you know they go from dam to dam because of high water and washouts. They never get comfortable due to thinking of the inevitable breaking up of the dam they toiled so hard to build. Fred W. sold a company and never enjoyed a penny of the fruits of his labor. He told me of the need to achieve some more wealth but primarily worried about losing it. He totally lived for hoarding his money. As fate would have it, he lost the money in a second business investment. He was so absorbed with the thought of losing it all, that ultimately he did. Have you ever noticed that what a person thinks is usually the dominating thought in their mind and the dominating outcome?

The lemmings are the business owners who sell companies and take too much advice from others. These people follow each other into the sea of destruction as lemmings do each spring, only to drown. The lemming type of post-business owner will take advice from his CPA, attorney, insurance adviser, financial planner, stockbroker, banker, and even his brother-in-law. Unfortunately, none of these people have built a business, met payroll, or been seriously concerned about the loss of all their assets.

I have seen a lot of lemming-type business owners end in poor financial condition from taking too much "good" advice. Business owners are often very good at determining what is right for them. More should heed their own advice.

As brilliant as most business builders are, they usually end in one of these categories. The greatest attribute of entrepreneurs is their ability to change. If they do make errors after selling, they can usually learn quickly from adverse experience.

XII

"Have I Got a Deal for You..."

One thing is certain for owners after selling their companies: Everyone has a deal for them! This new-found wealth brings out all the deal people. Hypes such as "50% on this" and "double your money on that" abound. They all have the right answers for investing the new wealth. If the sellers will just entrust them with their fortune, everything should be fine. This is the standard pitch, with variations on the theme. Oddly enough, many former business owners go for it. Having spent their entire work life building net worth, they re-invest in three weeks.

Constantly, I am reminded that the former owner made his money by founding and/or investing in business operations in which he had or acquired considerable knowledge and expertise. Most of the money that business owners have made is from their business. Investing in themselves was the logical and successful choice.

New money will always attract many people. Amazingly, people will find the new wealth no matter how hard those with new wealth try not to disclose information. In even the most closely held situations, people still find out where the former owner is and how to get in touch. One word of caution relating to the sharing of wealth: When either friends or relatives come knocking on the door for loans or advances, pass it up.

In a very high percentage of cases that I have witnessed relating to these types of loans, the results were disastrous. These friends and relatives typically pay you back last of all. A family member is easier to borrow from and much less onerous to deal with if it goes unpaid. Always watch for these types of loans to be trouble.

Professional consultants also play a part before and after the sale. A good CPA and tax attorney are great assets, but there comes a point when you must divorce yourself from their advice. I have witnessed firsthand a number of business owners who are somehow working for their CPA and attorney instead of vice versa. How could these people know more than you do about investing? They have never met payroll at large companies, leveraged assets, or invested large amounts of capital to get a return. These words have been spoken many times: "My advisor is against it." Why did he advise against it? Lack of knowledge or lack of understanding could be the reason. I do not mean to imply that having a working team is not important, but that you need to keep your advisors in perspective. They can be a tremendous help when it come to details. Your job is the big picture. Keep it in focus at all times. As a former business owner, you need to give yourself more credit. You are better at knowing and feeling what is right for you than anyone else.

Carl A. was in the food business in the southwest in the early 1980's. He sold the company and his advisor told him of the need to own tax-sheltered investments. He said it was imperative to own these investments, and Carl bought it all the way. The 1986 tax act came along and tax write-offs were no more. Ten years later he was still struggling to produce cash flow. Had he not listened to his advisor, his life would be totally different today.

Business owners are my consultants. In the last 15 years I have met and listened to over a thousand business owners. When I need advice or business help, these people are my greatest assets. They have seen almost every situation, from being broke to taking incredible chances to stay afloat. Business owners have wonderful people skills, compassion and understanding. They have had to be both tough and soft at times. Their knowledge is unbelievable.

If the former owner has a close relationship with his spouse, she can also help. She is the one person that knows him better than anyone else. His well-being and positive outcome are utmost in her mind. She paid a price for that success also. If he does not have a good relationship with his spouse, then he must make sure that he does have a confidant.

To sum up, business owners should remember their great traits. These characteristics are what got them to a level of unique financial success. They are their own best consultant. They are best advised to select carefully their professional investment consultants and analyze all major recommendations in detail. Caution is the watchword. Greed, indiscretion, and high risk are the cardinal sins of security investing and can quickly destroy a fortune that required decades to build.

XIII

$10 Million and Broke

Most people would ask how a business owner could sell out and end up losing one, five, ten, or fifteen million dollars. I admit it sounds rather unlikely. However, over the last twenty years I have seen a number of former business owners do just that. Their respect for how much money it is, and how hard it was to make, is just not there.

Owners who lose their post-sale money usually follow one of three patterns. The first is the owner who sells the company, for example, at five million dollars. He then thinks, "Five million — anyone can live on that." Taxes after the sale come to $1.5 million, leaving $3.5 million as principal. The business owner then buys a new beach house with all the trimmings for $650,000 and remodels his current home for $100,000. We are now down to $2,750,000. Both children hit up mom and dad for $100,000 of the new-found wealth. The new business entrepreneur (former owner) invests $1,200,000 in a new and totally unfamiliar business. We are now down to $1,350,000 liquid investment. The former business owner is having to take $200,000 per year out of principal to meet living expenses.

By the end of year three, we are down to $650,000 in liquid investment. The business in which he reinvested is not producing. If he does not get an income stream, his liquid capital will be gone in two to three years.

Of particular note here is the difference in first, second, and third generation wealth. Malcolm Forbes used to say "Shirtsleeves to shirtsleeves in three generations." The first generation builds it, the second generation sells it, and the third generation spends it. I am just as impressed with a second generation business builder who realizes what mental hurdles must be overcome to sell a business and to then maintain wealth as I am with the first generation entrepreneur. The group to which most of the risk goes is the third generation. They did not build, operate, or sell the business; therefore, money and wealth are often not appreciated.

The second type of business owner is the one who takes public stock for his company and decides to use part of the proceeds from the sale of the stock to pay off incidental debt and to invest the remaining balance. All of his friends show up with the deal of a lifetime. After investing in two or more risky and illiquid proposals, he confronts the April 15th tax deadline and the staggering capital gains tax on the sale of stock and interest burden on the loan obtained with stock as collateral. Over the course of time, the business deals go bad and no liquidity exists. The disastrous consequences are obvious: The fortune accumulated over a lifetime or decades is squandered and the former business owner becomes the unpaid servant of the IRS in order to liquidate the tax obligation, penalty, and interest payments.

The third type of owner who sells is the "has-to-be-in-business" person. After selling he is so lost and disoriented that jumping directly into another business is paramount in his mind. He cannot stand the thought of not being the boss. Over the years, I have observed so many of these people getting in the wrong business. Having to be *in* business was more important than the *right* business.

Wayne R. exchanged his portion of a partnership for stock in a publicly owned corporation. Although he was the number three partner and primarily successful because of the other two owners, he nevertheless received a substantial after-tax dollar amount for the sale of these shares. He immediately bought another business and over the next four years, I was witness to his total loss. My last correspondence with him was about an IRS tax lien letter!

My primary theory about these types of people is that their mind-set is a crucial variable. I have known a number of business owners who have sold companies and ended up broke. They seem to be very relaxed even after losing it all. In my opinion, they were never comfortable with a lot of money. They apparently had a difficult time seeing themselves as "rich." In fact, they spent so much time with their backs to the wall struggling with debt, compared to the fleeting era of fortune, that the former was a far more natural feeling. Their adrenaline flowed only with fear of failing. There was the feeling that nothing, even life, should be easy. The success attitude is much more important than one thinks. It involves a mode of thinking that makes a person feel "worthy" of success. There is no guilt or other negative feelings, only the belief that they *should* be wealthy and successful.

Not to be misunderstood, I have tremendous respect for business owners. Many of them establish or participate in a second or third business and do even better than in the first enterprise or at least operate profitable enterprises. Many of the sellers who lose all their money even do better the second time. Most of them do just fine. From my observation, only about five to ten percent end up in the manner previously mentioned. Obviously, it pays to be prudent, even after an initial, impressive success in business.

XIV

Security Is in the Mind

Everybody wants to feel financially secure! As a business owner you keep building for that security. After selling, you tend to think that security will now come. Cash in the bank, no debt, expenses of children gone, and no big obstacles. Life will now be so easy because problems disappear. But does this really happen? Only in the movies.

I have two stories I would like to share with you regarding security. The names will be changed to protect the innocent. John was the owner of a Southeastern service company that he sold to a public company. He received about two million dollars of value in stock and smartly sold enough to pay off all debt and put $500,000 in the bank. He and his wife were very frugal and wanted to be debt-free with about $800,000 of stock before paying the tax obligation. So they lived on the income from the CD's and watched for potential business deals.

I visited with them in 1987, 1988, and 1989, to discuss their financial situation. John and his wife felt very secure. He always reminded me that money cannot buy that feeling. He said he was perfectly happy playing golf in Florida and then coming home to Tennessee just to enjoy life. He wasn't worried about tomorrow. Living for today was enjoyable for both of them. In the winter they would go to their hunting cabin and stay for a few months. Essentially they lived on very little money, but were very secure mentally.

The recession brought a big real estate bust to the Southeast. John and his wife practically stole a house at 50% of value near a golf course in Tennessee. Biding their time was paying off. They would have gladly stayed in the old house had this opportunity not arrived.

They also had a chance to buy a glass company where both of them worked. This started providing more income, and then a new investment opportunity arrived. For $150,000 they were able to purchase 50% ownership of a car dealership. Each time I visited with them they displayed the same peaceful security. They thought $1.3 million was plenty to have, even if nothing worked out with these new ventures. They would be fine. My point is that $1.3 million is not that much money to live on. But it *was* all in their *minds*.

My next story involves Tom, who sold a service company in Texas and received about $30 million in cash. He had personally experienced excellent growth in the company he sold and expected to match those results in his own investing. Tom could not wait to start buying more companies and attain even larger net worth. He just felt as though his net worth of $25 million was not enough to be secure. He invested very heavily in two banks as well as in three or four other businesses. This was approximately 1979 — 1980 when most businesses in the Southwest were performing well.

Our discussions of investing in other areas were always too simple for him. He could not see getting to his *larger* goals by investing in a traditional manner. He was very impatient with the slow process of getting there. At that time, U.S. Treasury bonds were yielding over 12%, and the inflation rate was much higher. It was almost as though he felt "broke" with $25 million net worth.

Over the next six years he managed to lose all the money in the banks and most of the money in the businesses. The Southwest economy was bludgeoned during the early 1980's, as was his net worth.

I encountered Tom in 1986, when he was trying to get a small company started with a new patent. His net worth was probably no more than $1,000,000 liquid. He never found security.

Security is a state of mind. Everyone needs to be sensible with their assets through saving and investing, but there is a certain feeling that only comes from being comfortable within. What is security? What is enough? These questions can only be answered by each person. In the long run, there is only mental security. We all live, we all die; but we can only enjoy the comfort of financial security with highly individualistic definitions. For many, the foundation of that definition rests on frequently shifting sands.

XV

Purpose -
Everyone Needs It

The biggest question for most prior business owners becomes "What happens now?" After selling a company, the purpose of day-to-day activity gets blurred.
You thought your purpose was to build a company, sell
it, then reap the benefits afterwards. Then you find
that $2 million, $8 million, $25 million, or $50 million

is just that. All of the money doesn't necessarily provide the purpose you once had.

Former business owners are like professional athletes who face a somewhat similar stark reality of life after sports. You are not the boss anymore. You don't sign the checks or decide anything else for your company or employees. In many cases, you are just like your employees, only with more money, but without their employment.

Lack of purpose is something most business owners do not expect. They know there will be changes but not of this kind. The driving force to a big piece of their life is gone. Poof! No more! This is typically where people must do soul searching. What next? Pleasure? Work? Another business?

When consulting with clients, I can always tell when this point is reached. They start calling me very frequently and asking the same questions. They also start attending to detail much more than normal. The main reason is their lack of enough to do. Many spouses become very frustrated during this period. They ask why their partners can't get an office, go somewhere, occupy themselves in an avocation or community work.

This juncture in the former business owner's life becomes very critical. If he has a plan, then all may go well. If not, he must look within and find out what really makes him tick. Occasionally this is a first for him. Perhaps he owned a business for 25 years and only had to think of staying afloat.

What eventually happens is the realization that this business and maybe the next one or two are parts of the journey. There is no end; no winner and no loser. Just the privilege of getting to play.

Having watched owners sell companies for twenty years, I have noticed a true void when it comes to purpose. Most former owners have never even thought about the purpose of life. All of a sudden they are looking at a situation where money is no object and time no problem. Most never thought of this concept as a reality, only as a theory. While consulting with

business owners who have sold, a continual set of questions arise.

>Where did I come from?
>
>Where am I going?
>
>Is this all there is?
>
>What should I be doing now?

The purpose he once had of raising a family, building a company, or gaining net worth is gone. A new
purpose must be awakened in order for him to keep on
living. Without it, I feel certain their lives will be
shorter. With a new purpose, the former business owner
becomes invigorated and uplifted to move forward.
There are unlimited examples of persons in business,
politics, professions, and other sectors who have em-
barked on satisfying second "careers."

All things in life can be characterized with cycles:
religion, business, families, and nature. The job now is
to sow the seeds for a new cycle.

XVI

Happiness -
What's It All About?

Happiness, like financial security, is a very relative term, largely defined by the individual — ephemeral and often changing. Everyone describes happiness from his or her own perspective. I wrote this chapter because of the conflict that arises when someone sells a business and thinks happiness will arrive automatically.

For owners who were not ready to sell the business, happiness is getting started in a new business. For owners who were ready to sell the business, happiness may mean doing things they never thought of doing such as walking, painting, traveling, or doing very little. In the long run, happiness is in the mind. A state in happiness is always upbeat, forward thinking, and positive.

One of the happiest business owners I know lived in West Texas. He sold two different companies and ended up with a reasonable amount of money. He was always happy, even in the beginning when money was scarce. I noticed his relationship with his wife was always superior and the entire family got along amiably.

As he became more wealthy after selling other businesses and moving to Arizona, nothing changed. He stayed happy and the same was true of his entire family. He sold the businesses when they were ready to be sold. He also had a fine relationship with his employees and friends. Actually, money meant very little. His happiness was not built around the wrong ideas such as control, wealth, ego, and power. It was built around enjoying life and positive human relationships.

In contrast, I had a client in the Southeast who sold a company for a very large sum of money. His children were grown, and there was enough money to do anything he wanted.

But he was not happy when he had the business or after he sold the business. A very long divorce ensued, and for five years he was intent on controlling his ex-wife and the divorce. He spent millions of dollars on the outcome and still was not happy. For some reason he appeared to concentrate on being in a state of unhappiness. Money was no object, although he spent it in order to find happiness, which always eluded him.

Happiness is a state of mind just like all other states of mind. It is not bought but rather produced internally. The path a business owner takes after selling his company can leave him extremely happy or extremely sad.

Many business owners are happiest when running their business and managing operations about which they have gained some knowledge or expertise. One of the most disappointing meetings for me is a first-time interview with a business owner who should not have sold. He normally does not realize this mistake until sometime afterwards.

Many owners have told me how they regret having sold. They loved the day-to-day excitement and the control of their situation. Unfortunately, a larger company came along and made them an offer they thought they could not refuse. Only one problem — they confused money with happiness.

When contemplating selling his company, the owner should ask himself a few critical questions:

Does he relish his daily routine and its challenges? If so, then maybe he should think twice before selling. A year-round vacation may not be as satisfying.

Does he enjoy controlling a large organization and working towards long-term goals? If so, he should probably keep the company. After the sale it's only his family, money and friends. His world shrinks considerably.

Does he enjoy helping other people reach their goals? If so, maybe he is better off with a company where he can directly help people with their career goals.

In other words, selling a company is not always the "right thing" to do unless the offering price and net profit are the only criteria.

When contemplating selling, the owner must remember that happiness is a super achievement. He may be happiest managing his company. Only he can ask and answer the critical questions on this subject.

XVII

To Sell, or
Not to Sell

Months or even years after selling their entrepreneurial enterprises, many former owners begin to rethink their decisions to sell. The thought process is normal and almost all of them go through this retrospective experience at some time or another. Although most of these reflections are fleeting in nature, those owners who have not yet sold and are facing difficulties in reaching a decision, should consider some pertinent, practical factors, listed below.

In my opinion, 20% to 25% of all sellers should have retained control of their companies for two primary reasons. First is the loss of valuable personal monetary benefits or prerequisites. When the owner of a small company, valued at $2 million or less, sells, he surrenders all the tangible benefits connected with ownership, many of which are tax-free or partly tax-free — use of company autos, insurance (life and health), forms of tax-deferred income, and others which are included in the expenditures of the business operations.

When the small business owner sells, he usually receives a lump sum of cash or stock in the acquiring organization or some combination of the two. Creating the same life-style and level of living from these assets which the former owner and his family enjoyed can indeed be difficult. I have known many owners who failed to calculate how much capital was required to produce a cash flow stream equivalent to the magnitude of their remuneration plus benefits from the company which was sold. After-tax cash flow is the crux of spending ability.

If an owner has sold without fully considering the cash-flow feature, he should start searching for another business to acquire. Age is also a key factor, particularly if the seller is 40 to 50 years of age or younger. The replacement of cash flow can be projected another 35 years or more; and the sum must be adjusted to an inflation rate of 2.5% or more annually and federal/state income taxes as well. Obviously, the income stream is difficult to maintain, and the cost of living is usually higher than anticipated by heads of households. A huge pool of capital and reasonably good fortune with investments are essential. The owner who sells is often not aware of this fact until it is too late. The proceeds from the sale of the company seem large and ample at the outset, but shrink substantially compared to the former income and cash flow from the company.

The second reason to consider carefully before making a decision to sell is both mental and emotional. Many owners do not realize how centrally focused they are on managing the companies they have created. After selling their companies, they can lose their bearings, self importance, and esteem. In the beginning, they concentrate on sports, travel, and other projects they envisioned which freedom from business would allow, such as sharpening golf skills, fishing, and other avocations as a substitute. These surrogate occupations may last for only a few months before boredom and dissatisfaction dominate. Often the spouses must pay the penalty for the aimless wandering about the homestead, somewhat comparable to a lonely child without a playmate.

One characteristic I have observed in former owners is an almost frantic search to find something — almost anything constructive — to do. They check into business deal after business deal for possible purchase, franchise arrangements, consulting offers, and other opportunities. At some point, they reach the inevitable conclusion about the tragic error in selling their successful business operations — the essence of their lives and a kind of management-ego love affair. Unfortunately, this awakening is ex post facto and is, of course, too late to change.

The sole avenue of escape and change is to locate another business operation available for purchase with assets from the prior sale. This path, however, can be treacherous. Most former owners had knowledge and experience in a single specialized field of construction, manufacturing, retailing, services, or other area. Most of them have signed contracts for sales of their companies which include a long-term clause (usually five years or longer) for non-competition with the buyer. The disadvantages and risks of entering new fields of business are obvious.

The above two reasons should be carefully weighed before an owner makes an irreversible decision to sell his company. The ultimate decision is basically an enigma with no simple answers. A large business owner may receive huge liquid assets from a premium buyout but can feel lost and without purpose after the sale. A small owner may want out but cannot afford to sell at less than an adequate offering price. Owners must consider all ramifications, and the final decision may be determined by some sense of intuition. But the first and priority question should be: To sell, or not to sell?

XVIII

Sell or
Go Public ?

Most businesses reach the point where outside capital is indispensable for incremental growth. Either the business owner borrows the required funds or raises capital from the public investment market. One of the big choices that arises for the owner is this:

"My company is at a certain level of value. If I expand it in the public realm, it could be huge and I could be much wealthier. If the markets go bad and I fail, then my worth is greatly reduced. I know that I could also sell the business right now for a good price." The question becomes:

"Do I take the bird in the hand or risk it for more?"

I have seen some incredible success stories from people who decided on the public route. But they all had the personality type to be involved in a public company.

Business owners often dream of having their private company become a public company. They think of having their name associated with a public entity and the limelight that goes with it. Having access to unlimited capital also comes to mind. I have called on hundreds of former business owners who said they could have gone public but decided not to. I have also called on a number of former owners who wish they had gone public. What are the pros and cons of the decision to sell to another entity or to go public? Do they have the critical mass to go public? And lastly, are they the types of persons to run a public company? Hopefully I can provide some insight to these questions.

First of all, is the owner a seller or a builder? This is an extremely important question. If he is a seller, his priority is to raise the maximum amount of cash or cash and liquid securities. This mindset is the exact oppposite of the entrepreneur trying to build a public company. I notice this consistantly when companies go public with multiple founders whose long-term objectives are different. If an owner has the "selling out" mindset, he will never be comfortable with the long-term view needed to have a truly successful public company. Taking a company to the public market is a huge undertaking. It requires a complete commitment to build for the future. If an owner constantly thinks about when to "cash out," it will not work in the public realm.

XYZ Company was a service business put together in the Midsouth with multiple founders. They went public as planned and started to grow. I knew most of them and noticed their different approaches. A few of the founders were selfish and concentrated their efforts more on reselling than on the building concept. Inevitably, two years later the company had to be sold to another public company.

There is nothing "wrong" with being a seller or a builder. In fact, each role has its distinctive advantages and disadvantages. But each individual must discover to which group he belongs. If he is a seller, then he should enjoy starting and selling companies. If he is a builder, going public may be the answer.

The next item for consideration in deciding whether to sell or go public is personality. When the company is traded in the public market, the chief executive and other top ranking officers become fair game for everyone. Every move is scrutinized and every word is watched. It starts with investment bankers, public accounting firms, the Securities and Exchange Commission, trading exchanges, financial analysts, and all the way down to the smallest shareholder with ten shares who shows up at every annual meeting. The owner of a privately held company must ask himself if he can handle the scrutiny. If not, then he should attempt to sell his company instead of going public.

In the event an owner determines that his goals can only be met by going public with his company, and that he has the required personality, he has three options. First, locate the investment banking or other financial organization which can underwrite the initial public offering and work out all the financial, legal and other details for the prospectus for release by the underwriting team to potential buyers. Second, the owner may seek through an investment bank a public company which might be interested in buying a less than majority interest and willing to leave incumbent management in place. Third, the owner can grow his company by purchasing another company with related services or products and excellent growth prospects.

It should be emphasized that few entrepreneurs, as sole owners of their companies with absolute control of decision making, can truly visualize the year-to-year and often quarter-to-quarter pressures and strains which are concomitant with a consistent annual increase in net earnings of ten percent or more. When the growth target climbs above this level, it can rarely be sustained without additional acquisitions or mergers or through the development of new products and services. The shareholders and financial analysts are always in the background applying the pressure with high earnings expectations and the latter with highly suspect overly optimistic earnings predictions.

Ego also plays a huge role in selling or going public. Companies essentially go public to raise outside capital to make money for their shareholders in the future. But I have observed many companies in the public realm that were operated from the standpoint of the founder's ego. Many times that ego will get stepped on. The occasion may arise with the release of disappointing quarterly earnings for the first time, a major non-recurring loss for "restructuring," or heavy losses from a key product, service, or division. A CEO may wonder why pay this price for being public. When the owner has a private company, his decisions are supreme and nobody questions them. In the public realm, vulnerability to adverse criticism is multi-faceted. If the private owner's ego cannot take the constant pounding, he should sell his company and forget going public.

He must also determine if he really wants to confront the strains, tensions, and many tough decisions directly connected with managing a public company. The decision to go public is only the beginning of a tremendous undertaking. The maker of that decision should undergo keen self-analysis to be certain he is qualified for the task and its recurring challenges.

Last but not least is privacy. Many of the high net worth business owners we work with are very private and confidential. I have always gone above and beyond duty in my dealings with them to preserve this confidentiality.

But the financial privacy of a top officer in a publicly traded company is largely exposed in the public realm. The public has access to his share ownership, benefits, level of salary, and how many options he has. His whole life in regard to his company is an open book. He has to answer phone calls and questions from people that may not appeal to him. He is handcuffed when buying or selling stock, if acquired by the exercise of restricted options. The owner must also exercise extreme care when trading stock in his own company to avoid the appearance of acting on insider information. Such transactions must be recorded with the SEC and are widely reported in press by investment analysts who specialize in insider trading. And lastly, he has to deal with "Wall Street." This makes him just like a professional head coach. "What has he done for me lately?" If he does not perform, he must get ready for the heat. The Wall Street gang can be very cruel.

It comes down to size, need for capital, public or private, ego and risk. The owner must weigh all of these factors before deciding to sell or become a public company. Business owners have a sense of the best way to go in most cases. They have a keen sense of themselves and what is right in each situation. They must listen to themselves very carefully before committing to the public realm. In many cases, I have seen business owners sell out and be very glad that they did. In other cases, going to the public market was appropriate. Again, the self analysis must be keen and thorough before deciding on the public market.

Above are listed some of the pros and cons of going public versus selling the private company — egos, money, successes, and pitfalls. If all of this does not sound appealing, then the owner may want to sell his company instead of going public. A higher percent of owners of private companies obviously sell rather than go to the public markets. They understand that it is not their style. Others who do start public companies and often succeed go on to greatly enhancing the material welfare and security of everyone associated with them.

XIX

Investment Planning for the Future

After selling a company, the business owner will have new semi-liquid assets. They usually take the form of cash, stock, notes, or convertible bonds. In either case, the former owner has some investment planning to do. Over the years, I have met many owners who had failed to generate a three- to five-year plan. In almost all cases, no consideration was given to the need for taxable income, inflation, safety, or estate planning. The former business owner says, "I controlled my business and I can control my assets." The investment world may well allow him less control than his business did.

Our staff has always done a good job of creating plans for thirty-six to sixty months. Each former business owner is asked a number of questions about his vision of his future and his appetite for risks. Listed below are a few examples of questions asked to business owners after sale.

Can you be employed by someone else and be happy?

Do you plan a change in family status?

Will you be moving?

Have you made estate plans?

What has to happen over the next three years for you to feel good both personally and financially?

Will you be donating gifts periodically to the children?

Will you start another business?

Where will your office be located?

In most cases, business owners have always worked on their companies and not their personal investments. By asking some very direct questions, we can start to get down to the core. What makes this person happy? What's their purpose in life? Are they content?

Every business owner is usually working toward a goal when the business is growing. They can usually recite sales goals, profit and loss information and this month's numbers. But when asked about their personal investments and plans for next year, no answer is there. I ask a question of business owners after the sale. What exactly did you earn year to year on your investments? I have yet to have a business owner give me a percentage return on their investments. Why? They do not realize that this is their new business — managing their money! It is still return on equity, but now not in the business. It is still inventory turnover, but not in the business. It is still gross margins, but now not in the business.

A plan will allow the former owner to think about each area. Cash flow, taxes, costs, pre-tax and after-tax are all still factors in determining the plans.

The next part of the plan is to look back after two to three years and determine if goals have been achieved. Often, adjustments need to be made or goals changed. In order to invest for the future, more effort is needed than just meeting with four or five invest-ment people and choosing one. What are his asset types? Which assets are bulletproof? Detailed thinking and analysis are important to his investment health.

Most business owners are accustomed to paying themselves what they need while their business is pri-vate. After they sell, however, a great deal of thought must be given to determine the amount of cash flow needed for living expenses. The risk factors associated with their investments must also be calculated due to the need for consistent returns. Consideration must also be given to forecasting the capital requirements needed to start a new business. Unfortunately, these areas are often overlooked. They are much more important than most people realize.

Underestimating the value of planning is a classic mistake of former business owners. They tend to make all decisions on a "have to" basis. The idea is to have a nice flow of information and be prepared for all scenarios.

XX

Navigating the New Life

After selling a company, very few business owners have a road map for their immediate or long-term
future. First of all, a road map is hard to come by, if
they do not know their destination. Secondly, they need
to stop and think about the size of their assets. Thirdly,
they need to evaluate the adequacy of their assets in
coordination with career or retirement plans and the

requirement for minimum investment income for any selected style or level of living.

Many former business owners have never stopped to ask themselves what truly makes them happy. Is it engineering, managing, building, having free time, or a combination of all these?

Alan E. was a fifty-year-old owner of a textile business in the Southeast. He managed the company for twelve years and made a substantial profit at the time of sale. Prior to buying his original textile business, he worked for a competing company. I visited with him on two occasions. After the second visit, I told him he would probably not be an investor with us. "Why do you say that?" he asked. My response was that he *loved* running his own company. That was his passion in life. He would buy another company and therefore would need to keep his assets in cash or equivalents. Sure enough, it happened within two years.

You may also be inclined to be a builder or engineer. If this is the case, your spouse may be in for a long painful period until you get another company in the construction or manufacturing sector. John B. was a builder of machines in the Midwest and had many patents in the company he sold. After selling the company, I met with him and his wife and set up an investment plan for a secure and comfortable retirement. In the back of my mind, I knew he would have problems due to his insatiable appetite for building things. He assured me that this was not the case, so we put his money to work for a conservative future.

Just as I had suspected, he started a new company within three years under a schedule of four payments. Ultimately, we had to liquidate many of his investments for this business. After this financial obligation was completed, he had very little liquidity left. However, he was fully aware of his new career and objectives and happy with them. This move was carefully planned, not a spur-of-the-moment decision.

Other business owners know that retirement from day-to-day business is what they want. They want no employees, no payroll, no taxes, and no lawsuits. Bill L. is a fine person with whom I have done business for fifteen years. He moved to Florida after having sold a company in another state. He loves every day and plans everything around his wife and their leisure and recreational activities. Leaving the business world behind was great for him. Playing golf, traveling, and cultivating friendships are his interests. I could sense this immediately about him and verified that it was true.

The second aspect of navigating the new life is size of assets. A business owner may take $200,000 to $500,000 per year from a business for personal living expenditures and not even realize it. Most people do not understand the benefit of being able to produce large cash flows year after year. Very few business owners stop to think about what size of assets are needed to produce certain levels of income. Our group has always categorized owners after a sale depending on the size of their assets. On the following page are listed the basic asset levels after selling a company.

Size of Assets

1. $	500,000	- $	1,000,000
2.	1,000,000	-	3,000,000
3.	3,000,000	-	10,000,000
4.	10,000,000	-	25,000,000
5.	25,000,000	-	50,000,000
6.	50,000,000	-	100,000,000
7.	100,000,000	-	250,000,000
8.	250,000,000	-	over

If an owner sold his company for three million or less, he may have trouble producing the personal cash flow he was accustomed to. Our experience has tracked certain characteristics of the different levels. Here are some examples.

A very high percentage of sellers for one million dollars or less spend the money in a brief period of time and of necessity have to return to the work place in some capacity.

The one million to three million dollar sellers will have to be much more frugal than they had expected due to the life-style to which they had become accustomed. The business produced more cash flow than their assets will.

After the sale of assets producing four to ten million dollars, the former owners will usually be able to produce a cash flow from investment income to equal their life-styles as entrepreneurs. Even so, this group needs to be prudent. If they make one or two sizable bad investments their actual and emotional financial security may alter dramatically.

Sellers who receive ten million to twenty-five million dollars should have a life of luxurious living as long as they do not invest a huge sum of their cash assets in one security only to see it collapse in value before they can liquidate. Problems in this category have usually arisen when the persons were concentrated in investments that were not well researched and analyzed. I have witnessed the fortunes of a number of people drop drastically from twenty million to five million due to a single risky investment.

The sellers of company assets in the range of twenty-five million to fifty million dollars are fewer in number and usually can absorb a couple of serious investment mistakes. This magnitude of assets generally allows time for recovery, provided future investment decisions are conservative.

The number of sellers who receive from fifty million to one hundred million dollars is very small. At this level they understand that risk is not needed for anything. What else can they buy? If they want more money, then it is the game that matters, not the money.

Those sellers who receive one hundred million to two hundred fifty million dollars for their companies are very few and can demand and pay for the best of services and goods. They know the power of their fortune, even if they play it down mentally. They tend to make life very simple again.

The owners of companies who liquidate for two hundred and fifty million dollars and above are so private that information about them is hard to find. We meet them through referrals or private transactions. Privacy becomes very important to this group. Cash flow becomes a reverse problem. Where do they invest it?

Each seller of a business should realize that adequacy is relative. What constitutes enough is different for each person. Navigating the future will depend heavily on the total value of assets at any given time. Each seller should think about that concept as a sine qua non which requires periodic review.

Much time is needed after selling a company to decide what to do and when to take action. The seller should not rush, but should keep his mind clear, and consider carefully all facets of each major monetary decision.

XXI

Enjoy the Ride

When all the checks and stock are exchanged, and assets transferred after selling, you are back to square one. Hopefully some of the information in this book will help you decide which course is best. In any case, life goes on and changes occur.

My personal observations about business owners who sell companies are as follows: Business owners are the greatest group of people to work with in the world.

They understand risk, reward, and achievement. Most all of them have had periods of high stress, serious setbacks, and great excitement. They are of an optimistic nature, always believing that the good and the positive will prevail. By and large, they are honest and endowed with high moral character. Of course, there are a few with negative character traits. Nevertheless, entrepreneurial business owners are the true builders of the economic foundation of this great country, the essential twins of political and personal freedom. Unfortunately, they get very little thanks for taking the risk to build a business and put their personal savings and credit ratings on the line.

After they sell their companies, my wish for them is to have great mental and financial security. When counseling and managing investments for former business owners, we constantly stress the idea of "peace of mind."

What difference does it make if he sold for four million dollars and somebody else got thirty million dollars for their company? As a business owner, he probably grew much bigger than he had expected. Even if he lives to be 110 years old, life can seem short. Comparing himself or wanting to "beat" someone at the money game leaves a very empty feeling when all is said and done. Trying to pass the other person or competitor only takes the attention off oneself.

Through experiences of observing owners, the truly happy ones had "peace of mind." In my opinion, success lies in knowing you did the best you could do in every situation with the tools and resources available. A lifetime teacher who touches the lives of many children growing up is just as successful as Sam Walton of Wal-Mart. Who is to say that dollars of net worth is the only guideline?

Over the last twenty years I have seen former business owners render varied kinds of personal services for others. One of my customers and friends in North Carolina recently helped his maid by paying off the debt her church owed. Another client in California helps everyone he comes in contact with to achieve their goals (his secretary, yardman, maid, children, high school friends, and just about anybody he can help).

Jack B. was a fantastic businessman who sold his company and set up foundations and charitable gifts of all sorts. He was a tough guy to deal with but had a heart as generous as sugar is sweet. He gave money to great causes and never looked for recognition. The ability to help people was what he most enjoyed.

My good friend and mentor who helped me write this book has always said that helping people while you can still see them benefit in life is much more rewarding than bequests after death. Most former owners of businesses practice this in some form or other. They give to people quietly without needing recognition or fanfare. In December of each year my staff is inundated with requests by clients to transfer money to charities. All are people who are giving back something they feel was given to them.

Having "net worth" allows the person the ability to help others and therefore gain incredible "self-worth." Many former owners are helping people to become the best they can be. The return on this investment is great self-esteem and enduring satisfaction for the former business owner. The purpose as mentioned in Chapter XIII comes into focus. This new world of liquidity offers the benefit to start new ventures by investing in others to help them be the best they can be. It must be done in a way that does not deprive the recipient of self-worth also. The people a person invests in must feel they are contributing to their own success — not just having money from an outside investor. A certain way of helping others to become the best they can be is important. For the new you, this almost becomes the next business. It also becomes the self-worth that replaces many things that happened in the former business.

Most of the former business owners are spreading "good deeds" after selling. In the end, good work and helping people is the most lasting legacy. Remember, the journey is just a ride and success is just an ongoing part of that. Too many people get caught up in the wrong purposes in life only to realize it too late. Build the business, sell the business, start over, retire. Whatever you do: Enjoy the ride!

Epilogue

As time moves forward, there will be more and more people selling companies. They will either elect to retire or to continue working with other ventures. I hope some of the information in this book will benefit all those who read it. I am greatly indebted to all the people who have helped me along my journey. My gratitude goes out to all of the business owners and their knowledge from which I have gained. The path to the future changes for the business owner after selling. I believe, however that the emotional paths will be the same no matter what the circumstances.

Life is indeed a journey, and one hopes that after a business owner sells his company, he can better understand this fact. It is a journey made up of doing business, helping others, family, and achievement. Nothing is more exciting than to watch a business owner achieve success after selling the company. In sharp contrast, it is also true that nothing is sadder than to see a business owner lost after selling. There is more to life than the company. The owners who realize this go on to the next plateau in life with ease. The others never seem to realize that the trip was meant to be enjoyed for what it was.

Many thanks go out to those who helped me in this endeavor, including Frank Knapp, Penelope Penland, Sue Noel, John Keys, Kathy Prince, James Bruton, Hal Holmes, and all the many business owners I have known.

Should you read this book and sell your company sometime in the future, I hope the information you obtained here will help. Best of luck to all who have sold and to all who will be selling their companies in the future!

- Ted Oakley